COMPUTER SCIENCE

SCIENCE 24/7

ANIMAL SCIENCE

CAR SCIENCE

COMPUTER SCIENCE

ENVIRONMENTAL SCIENCE

FASHION SCIENCE

FOOD SCIENCE

HEALTH SCIENCE

MUSIC SCIENCE

PHOTO SCIENCE

SPORTS SCIENCE

TRAVEL SCIENCE

SCIENCE 24/7

COMPUTER SCIENCE

JANE P. GARDNER

SCIENCE CONSULTANT:
RUSS LEWIN
SCIENCE AND MATH EDUCATOR

Mason Crest

Mason Crest
450 Parkway Drive, Suite D
Broomall, PA 19008
www.masoncrest.com

Printed and bound in the United States of America.

Series ISBN: 978-1-4222-3404-4
Hardback ISBN: 978-1-4222-3407-5
EBook ISBN: 978-1-4222-8491-9

First printing
1 3 5 7 9 8 6 4 2

Produced by Shoreline Publishing Group LLC
Santa Barbara, California
www.shorelinepublishing.com
Cover Photograph: Dreamstime.com/Monkey Business Images

Library of Congress Cataloging-in-Publication Data
Gardner, Jane P., author.
        Computer science / by Jane P. Gardner ; science consultant: Russ Lewin, science department chairman, Santa Barbara Middle School.
        pages cm. -- (Science 24/7)
        Includes bibliographical references and index.
ISBN 978-1-4222-3407-5 (hardback) -- ISBN 978-1-4222-3404-4 (series) -- ISBN 978-1-4222-8491-9 (ebook) 1. Computer science--Juvenile literature. 2. Application software--Juvenile literature.
I. Title.
QA76.23.G37 2016 004--dc23
                                    2015014792

IMPORTANT NOTICE
The science experiments, activities, and information described in this publication are for educational use only. The publisher is not responsible for any direct, indirect, incidental or consequential damages as a result of the uses or misuses of the techniques and information within.

Contents

KEY ICONS TO LOOK FOR

Words to Understand: These words with their easy-to-understand definitions will increase the reader's understanding of the text, while building vocabulary skills.

Sidebars: This boxed material within the main text allows readers to build knowledge, gain insights, explore possibilities, and broaden their perspectives by weaving together additional information to provide realistic and holistic perspectives.

Series Glossary of Key Terms: This back-of-the-book glossary contains terminology used throughout this series. Words found here increase the reader's ability to read and comprehend higher-level books and articles in this field.

INTRODUCTION

Science. Ugh! Is this the class you have to sit through in order to get to the cafeteria for lunch? Or, yeah! This is my favorite class! Whether you look forward to science or dread it, you can't escape it. Science is all around us all the time.

What do you think of when you think about science? People in lab coats peering anxiously through microscopes while scribbling notes? Giant telescopes scanning the universe for signs of life? Submersibles trolling the dark, cold, and lonely world of the deepest ocean? Yes, these are all science and things that scientists do to learn more about our planet, outer space, and the human body. But we are all scientists. Even you.

Science is about asking questions. Why do I have to eat my vegetables? Why does the sun set in the west? Why do cats purr and dogs bark? Why am I warmer when I wear a black jacket than when I wear a white one? These are all great questions. And these questions can be the start of something big . . . the start of scientific discovery.

1. **Observe:** Ask questions. What do you see in the world around you that you don't understand? What do you wish you knew more about? Remember, there is always more than one solution to a problem. This is the starting point for scientists—and it can be the starting point for you, too!

Enrique took a slice of bread out of the package and discovered there was mold on it. "Again?" he complained. "This is the second time this all-natural bread I bought turned moldy before I could finish it. I wonder why."

2. **Research:** Find out what you can about the observation you have made. The more information you learn about your observation, the better you will understand which questions really need to be answered.

Enrique researched the term "all-natural" as it applied to his bread. He discovered that it meant that no preservatives were used. Some breads contain preservatives, which are used to "maintain freshness." Enrique wondered if it was the lack of preservatives that was allowing his bread to grow mold.

3. **Predict:** Consider what might happen if you were to design an experiment based on your research. What do you think you would find?

Enrique thought that maybe it was the lack of preservatives in his bread that was causing the mold. He predicted that bread containing preservatives would last longer than "all-natural" breads.

4. **Develop a Hypothesis:** A hypothesis is a possible answer or solution to a scientific problem. Sometimes, they are written as an "if-then" statement. For example, "If I get a good night's sleep, then I will do well on the test tomorrow." This is not a fact; there is no guarantee that the hypothesis is correct. But it is a statement that can be tested with an experiment. And then, if necessary, revised once the experiment has been done.

Enrique thinks that he knows what is going on. He figures that the preservatives in the bread are what keeps it from getting moldy. His working hypothesis is, "If bread contains preservatives, it will not grow mold." He is now ready to test his hypothesis.

5. **Design an Experiment:** An experiment is designed to test a hypothesis. It is important when designing an experiment to look at all the variables. Variables are the factors that will change in the experiment. Some variables will be independent—these won't change. Others are dependent and will change as the experiment progresses. A control is necessary, too. This is a constant throughout the experiment against which results can be compared.

Enrique plans his experiment. He chooses two slices of his bread, and two slices of the bread with preservatives. He uses a small kitchen scale to ensure that the slices are approximately the same weight. He places a slice of each on the windowsill where they will receive the same amount of sunlight. He places the other two slices in a dark cupboard. He checks on his bread every day for a week. He finds that his bread gets mold in both places while the bread with preservatives starts to grow a little mold in the sunshine but none in the cupboard.

6. **Revise the hypothesis:** Sometimes the result of your experiment will show that the original hypothesis is incorrect. That is okay! Science is all about taking risks, making mistakes, and learning from them. Rewriting a hypothesis after examining the data is what this is all about.

Enrique realized it may be more than the preservatives that prevents mold. Keeping the bread out of the sunlight and in a dark place will help preserve it, even without preservatives. He has decided to buy smaller quantities of bread now, and keep it in the cupboard.

This book has activities for you to try at the end of each chapter. They are meant to be fun, and teach you a little bit at the same time. Sometimes, you'll be asked to design your own experiment. Think back to Enrique's experience when you start designing your own. And remember—science is about being curious, being patient, and not being afraid of saying you made a mistake. There are always other experiments to be done!

1
COMPUTER
COMMUNICATIONS

Just great. Hugo looked at his schedule. His last class of the day was a computer class. *The absolute last thing I want to learn is how to write computer code.*

It was the first day of school and Hugo's first day in his new school. He and his mother had moved to town a few weeks before and had just managed to unpack. He didn't know any of the kids here, and they all seemed to know each other. He had managed to get through most of his first day—but was now faced with a computer class.

As soon as Hugo settled into a seat at the back of the room, the teacher, a youngish man, wearing a button-down shirt with the sleeves rolled up, wrote his name on the board: "Mr. Dewey."

"Welcome to a new computer class here at North High School. You can think of yourselves as guinea pigs," he said. "Computers have never been taught exactly like this, and I'll be honest, I really had to convince the administration that this was a course worth teaching. So," Mr. Dewey paused—"do a good job, my job depends on it!"

Students in the class giggled nervously and looked at each other. They hadn't anticipated this sort of introduction. A few students jumped in their seats when Mr. Dewey clapped his hands.

"Okay, then. I'd like you to break into pairs and head to one of the tables at the back of the room. We'll be using the computer stations later on, possibly tomorrow."

This is what Hugo had dreaded. The grouping up when everyone knew each other already. He looked and saw a girl waving toward him. "Come over here," she mouthed.

Hugo moved to the back of the room. The girl stuck out her hand. "I'm Chloe. You're new here, aren't you? I saw you in my English class."

"I'm Hugo. And yeah, I just moved here with my mom a few weeks ago."

Mr. Dewey brought their attention back to the class. "Over the next week or so, your group will be starting a business. Well, more accurately, your group will be setting up the communications necessary for your company." He told the students more about what he expected.

Hugo took notes but leaned over toward Chloe. "I thought we were going to be programming and writing code and dealing with HTML stuff. This isn't at all what I expected."

She nodded. "I know. This is much more interesting. Shh, what is he saying?"

Over the next week Hugo and Chloe worked on their company. They decided that their company would sell a specialized treat made for cats. They knew that if they were going to be successful in their business, they would need to have a presence on the Internet.

Chloe looked at her notes. "Okay, Hugo. You can be in charge of developing the Web page. We need a dynamic Web page for our company."

"That's right," he said. "And I've been thinking about that. I have been searching some Web sites on my own, trying to find out what makes some of them good and some of them totally lame. And yes, before you say it, I do realize that is a matter of opinion."

"Good, I'm glad you get that. But what have you found?" Chloe urged him along.

"Well, I would want us to have a page with our products, a way for someone to search the database, and information about the ingredients."

"I think we should have a page with testimonials, too," suggested Chloe, "so people who are thinking of ordering can see what others think."

Hugo was rapidly taking notes as she talked. "And we need to be able to have a shopping cart feature and need a

Words to Understand

HTML Stands for hypertext markup language—this is the code that creates most standard Web pages.

Intranet a network that is dedicated to one company and can only be accessed by those within the company

space to input credit card and shipping rates," brainstormed Hugo. "Man, I am glad I don't really have to make this Web site. Designing it on paper is complicated enough."

"Okay, now what about connecting to social media?" Chloe asked.

Hugo looked at his notes. "I've decided we need to hit up a bunch of sites. Instagram, Twitter, and Pinterest to name a few. If we have photos of cats eating our treats along with some testimonials and links to our Web site, I think we could be pretty successful on those sites."

Chloe agreed. "Great. We would also need to have someone monitoring traffic on those sites and updating them frequently so they don't get old."

"I've been looking at what our offices will need," Chloe continued. "We need to have emails that are associated with our Web site, of course. I also expect that we will need to have some sort of **Intranet**."

"What's that?" Hugo asked.

"It's a communication system that a company uses internally. It will help set up things like phone lines as well as let us keep our files and contacts and order forms securely within the company."

Mr. Dewey leaned in over Hugo's shoulder. "I really like what I am hearing over here. You two recognize that a 21st century business is grounded in technology. But that sometimes, the more traditional technologies get overlooked."

Hugo smiled. "Thanks. This isn't what I thought this class was going to be like at all."

"Whew," Mr. Dewey said, wiping his hand across his brow. "I am glad to hear that! Who wants to write code all day?"

The Internet

Believe it or not, the Internet has been around for a long time. It all started in 1958 when the U.S. Department of Defense started the Advanced Research Projects Agency. This agency started a network of mainframe computers at major universities across the United States in 1969 and the Internet was born. Many people, though, confuse the Internet with the World Wide Web. The World Wide Web was proposed in 1989 and it was meant to be another way to transmit data over the Internet. Until then, navigating the Internet was cumbersome and not "user-friendly." The World Wide Web was the beginning of the Internet as we all know it—starting with the first Web site created in 1990.

Try It Yourself

Have you ever set up your own Web site? Is there something you would like to show the world online? Do you have an interest in a particular sport, or a type of music, or would you like to set up a business? How about setting up a Web site to showcase yourself to the world.

Materials:
- notebook
- pen and pencil
- Internet access

1. Decide what you want to showcase on your Web site. Is it your stats on the baseball team? Your collection of model cars? Or an idea for a new business?

2. Do your research. Search the Internet for Web sites that are showcasing or offering similar things that you want to. What do you like about those sites? What would you change?

3. Start to map out your Web site. Keep in mind you'll need to have different pages. Perhaps you'll want to have a "contact" page. Maybe you'll need an order form. Or a "leave a comment" box. Get your ideas down on paper. How will your Web site flow?

Note: Download a free Web site-building program. Set it up. With your grown-up's permission, publish it online. Be sure to include a "hit counter" so you can see how many people travel to your site!

2
COMPUTERS
IN CARS

Monday afternoon, Mr. Dewey presented the class with a PowerPoint presentation that began with an automobile. "You all did a great job on your business communications project. But it's time to move on. We're now going to spend some time talking about computers and automobiles."

Mr. Dewey challenged his class to brainstorm different examples of the use of computers in automobiles. They spent some time comparing their lists and then he opened it up for discussion.

Hugo was one of the first students to raise his hand. "Computers have helped with diagnosing troubles and problems with car engines and other components."

"Yes, yes! Great one," Mr. Dewey said, adding the words "diagnostic tool" to the board. "What else?"

Another student raised his hand. "I saw a commercial on TV last night where a car was parallel parking itself."

Mr. Dewey scribbled that down as well. "Excellent. I want to talk more about **autonomous** cars later, so that will be on the list."

"What about **GPS**?" suggested Chloe. "And hands-free technologies for phones and radios and the Internet."

"Slow down a bit. This is all great stuff. GPS is pretty much standard in cars now. Until recently, people used portable GPS devices that they plugged into their car. And really not that long ago, people carried maps around."

The class came up with more examples and the discussion continued. After a while, Mr. Dewey put down the marker and asked the class a question. "What do you think about these? Is technology used for convenience? Or for safety?"

A silence fell over the room while the students thought. Hugo cautiously raised his hand. "I think most of these are ultimately focused on safety. Sure, you can argue that having a GPS is a convenience. Or that being able to answer your phone without using your hands is a convenience, but isn't it really a matter of safety?"

Mr. Dewey and some of the other students were nodding as Hugo spoke. "I agree with you. Even the technology that is used to diagnose problems with the engine or to calculate gas mileage has safety implications. Good observation, Hugo."

Mr. Dewey continued. "Let's look at those self-driving, or autonomous, cars for a second."

He put up an image of a car that looked pretty much like any other car that might be driving around the block. Maybe a little sleeker, a little more streamlined, but nothing dramatic. There was also a device mounted on the roof. A shot of the car's interior showed a large computer screen near the passenger seat and some strange-looking controls.

"This car uses three things: a laser scanner, a GPS, and a series of cameras," Mr. Dewey explained. "These three devices are hooked up to the car's com-

Words to Understand

autonomous able to be operated without direct human control

electromagnetic radiation the waves of light energy across the magnetic spectrum, including visible, X-rays, and more

GPS Global Positioning System, the series of satellites used to track positions on Earth

laser an intense, focused beam of light used in this case to "read" information for the computer

puter and work together to allow the car to navigate safely through complex courses.

"Up here on the roof of the car is the laser sensor. This scans the area around the car constantly. The laser hits objects, and bounces back to the sensor to estimate how far away the objects are."

"Isn't that how a bat does it?" piped in Chloe.

Mr. Dewey nodded. "Basically, but a bat uses reflected sound waves, called echolocation. Bats use sound waves of up to 100,000 hertz—ultrasound—to navigate and hunt. They send out ultrasound waves, which bounce off distant objects and travel back to their ears. This tells the bat how far away objects are so they can avoid obstacles or catch the mosquitos they are after.

"This laser uses light. In fact, the word "laser" isn't actually a word—it represents the phrase *light amplification by stimulated emission of radiation*. In other words, light becomes stronger when it is exposed to electromagnetic radiation."

He pointed at the device on top of the car. "The laser is constantly monitoring the distances between objects and the car. There is a GPS, of course, which pinpoints the exact location of the car on a map. Other equipment, like cameras, help keep the passengers, and others on the road, safe. Technology has really changed the way we drive."

Autonomous Cars–a Good Thing?

Proponents of the self-driving car cite many reasons why this car is a good thing. Studies suggest that autofocus cars would reduce the number of traffic accidents–computers make fewer mistakes than humans. Autonomous cars could reduce traffic jams and make the roads flow more smoothly. And, these vehicles could open up a whole new world for those who can't drive now–underage drivers, the elderly, the blind, and physically challenged. There are those doubters, however, who suggest that autonomous cars would lead to the loss of many jobs for those who drive vehicles for a living, there would be a lack of privacy, and that many drivers would be hesitant to give up their control of the cars. We'll have to see what the future brings.

Try It Yourself

How difficult would it be to program a vehicle to drive you where you want to go? There are many programs today that do that work for you. But what if you had to do it the old way—by hand? Try to come up with precise directions to lead a friend to a new location. Do you think they would get there?

Materials:
- notebook
- compass
- tape measure
- paper and pencil
- a friend

1. With a friend, measure your pace. Walk ten steps along a hallway. Use your normal steps. Measure the distance you walked. Divide by 10—that's your average pace.

2. Use your pace measurement and a directional compass to create a step-by-step map of a small area (perhaps a playground, or the route from your science class to the cafeteria, via the library). Make a route with many turns and obstacles. Be very specific in your directions.

3. Have your friend follow your directions exactly. They should note where they go and where they run into trouble. Did your instructions send them into a wall? Or the wrong way? They should follow your directions as accurately as possible, while remaining safe.

4. How did it go? How successful were your directions? What do you think now about the power of a digital map?

3
APPS

Mr. Dewey stood in front of the class. "Let's just say, for the sake of argument, that you were allowed to use your phones in class. What apps would I find on your phone?"

The students all began to call out different things that they had on their phone.

Mr. Dewey held up his hand. "Okay, okay. I get it. You have apps for your music, apps to track your exercise, to keep track of your allowance, and even apps to monitor your homework. But, did you realize that apps haven't always been around? Back in my day, we had to use notebooks, and pencils, and calendars, to keep track of all the things you do on your phone right now."

Hugo raised his hand. "Gee, how old are you, Mr. Dewey?" After the class stopped laughing, Mr. Dewey continued. "Funny, Hugo. But seriously, apps, or computer applications, are basically just a software program—a special software program, though. Most of what we now think of as apps are actually mobile applications. They are designed for use on a mobile device such as a phone or a tablet. There are also apps that are designed and used on desktop computers."

"What is an example of a desktop computer app?" asked Chloe.

"I know," another student answered before Mr. Dewey could. "That would be software that you access and use while you are online, rather than something from your desktop."

Words to Understand

apps short for applications, programs that run on mobile devices or computers

software code that operates computers

"That's right," Mr. Dewey continued. "Online apps are cheaper and in many ways more efficient than using traditional software. A company, for example, may use online apps to do things like manage their inventory or for invoicing or for email. And there are programs to help create documents and spreadsheets available this way, too."

Hugo raised his hand. "And the mobile apps?"

"The mobile apps are what we have become more used to," Mr. Dewey explained. "Mobile apps are used for businesses, too. In fact, business has changed significantly in the past few years as apps take over. Sending photos, tracking packages, signing documents, all these things can be done using an app. It's amazing.

Everything from signing for a package to ordering pizza has become available as an app.

"So now, I want you all to make an app. I know some of you are really concerned about writing code here in this class," he snuck a look directly at Hugo and smiled, "but we have many ways to do this. First things first, though—I want you to come up with an idea for your app. Talk with your partner, see if you can come up with a good one."

Hugo and Chloe looked at each other and got out their notebooks. Hugo hoped this wasn't going to be too bad.

Chloe was excitedly writing notes. "I want to develop an app that will keep kids brushing their teeth for the proper amount of time. My little brother is notorious for doing a poor job brushing. I had a toothbrush once when I was really little that buzzed every 30 seconds, telling me to switch to a different quadrant of my mouth. I think if I made an app that did something like that, while playing music or flashing images, it could be a hit."

"Why don't you play music with a certain beat so the kid can brush his teeth at a reasonable rate?" Hugo added.

"Great idea. What are you going to do?"

"I have no ideas," Hugo admitted. "I guess I want to see what it entails first."

Over the next week, Mr. Dewey led the students through an online program to develop an app. The program they used didn't require any programming or HTML skills. There were icons and features that they were able to drag and drop into a program. It wasn't the most sophisticated program, but Mr. Dewey showed the students the basics and helped them see the limitations of the program.

"I hope," Mr. Dewey said at the end of the app project, "that you all see now how it really is difficult to write an app that people want to use. Lots of people do it, but only a few can develop an app that will be used by many."

The Cost of Apps

If you check out an app store on your mobile device, you'll most likely find many free apps. But you have probably heard stories about people getting rich by writing an amazing app. How does this happen? There are several ways, and keep in mind that the number of people getting rich is very low. But getting sponsors, selling ads, and having locked features on your app that people need to purchase as an upgrade are all ways this can happen. Good luck!

Try It Yourself!

Is there something you would like to write an application for? Perhaps you have thought of some quick time-saving technique. Or maybe you have an idea how to organize your notes from math class or a comic book collection. Try your hand at writing an app. Who knows, it might actually turn into something big!

Materials:
- notebook
- pen and pencil
- Internet access

1. Explore different applications on your phone or on the Internet. What sort of things do apps do for the user?

2. What type of app would you create? One that helps people? One that is more for entertainment? Jot down your ideas.

3. Make a list of the things you would like your app to be able to do. Find apps that provide a similar service and note the things you would like to have in yours. Do you have any new ideas?

4. Take a stab at writing the application. Be sure to be systematic and don't skip steps.

Take it further:
Find a Web site on the Internet that explains how to write an app. There are many, some even claiming to teach you in two hours how to do it. Try one or more of them out with your idea. How did it turn out? Be sure to test your app, and then test it again and again!

19

4
HEALTH AND COMPUTERS

Mr. Dewey split his seventh period computer class into small groups. "I want each group to search the Internet to find ways that the health care industry uses technology. I have five different topics—each group will get a topic. They are: personal health apps, managing prescriptions, imaging and diagnostic tools, tracking outbreaks, and linking doctors to patients and other doctors."

Hugo's group chose looking into technology linking doctors with their patients and other doctors. Chloe's group got to report on using technology to track outbreaks. Mr. Dewey explained that each group would be presenting their findings in a PowerPoint presentation by the end of the week.

The students began their research. Hugo was amazed at all the advances in health care technology. He knew that things had changed, but he had no idea what this actually meant for patients around the world.

He found that now many doctors and health care facilities allow patients to access their records through a special, password protected Web site. These "portals" allow patients and doctors to communicate. This includes everything from scheduling an appointment or asking to refill a prescription, to general information about a follow-up exam or interpretation of lab results.

Hugo made himself a note to ask his mother if she had signed up for this. It seemed to him to be a good idea. Doctors who had commented on it indicated that it made them feel more connected to their patients and helped them prepare for future office visits.

On the day of the presentations, Chloe's group was prepared. They had looked at the way that technology had been used in recent years to track the Ebola outbreak and a particularly bad strain of the flu. Their findings were impressive.

"As you can see here," Chloe said, pointing to a map of Africa, "the recent Ebola outbreak started in a village in Guinea. A small boy died of Ebola in December of 2013, and it began to spread.

"This particular outbreak of Ebola was amazing," Chloe continued. " Tragic, and amazing. The spread of the virus was actually traced with the use of social media. Never before in the history of medicine had this happened."

Another member of her group took over. "Web sites, such as HealthMap, developed and maintained by a group of scientists in Boston, Massachusetts, use computers to follow the outbreak. Computer programs were written to read thousands and thousands of social media sites, news sites, and government Web sites. Any mention of Ebola, or hemorrhagic fevers, or the like were tracked and traced."

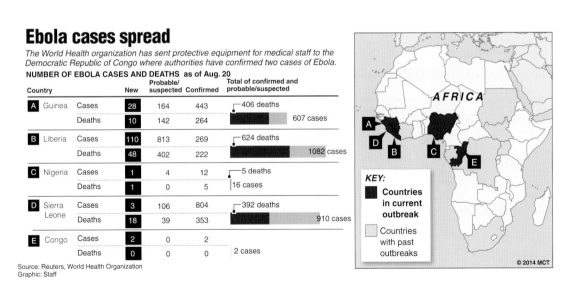

Computer data helps generate infographics like this, which can help people understand the spread of diseases.

"Wow," said Mr. Dewey, "that is pretty impressive. What else did you find?"

Chloe pointed to a different map. "Similar things are happening here in the United States with less deadly diseases. A recent flu outbreak was tracked on Twitter. People complain about being sick to their friends and followers on sites like Twitter or Facebook. That data is analyzed and used by scientists to track the outbreak. The scientists are also monitoring information from doctor's offices, clinics, and hospitals as well."

"And," another student chimed in, "the CDC—Centers for Disease Control and Protection—and several major universities in the United States are developing apps that can help with the mapping of the disease. If you have the flu, for example, you can download the app. On it you can input information about symptoms, temperatures, and the length of the disease. All the more data to help scientists figure out things like vaccines and severity of the outbreak."

Mr. Dewey was pleased with his students. "We are starting to see some very powerful uses of computers for our health and well-being. And it's only going to keep growing."

Gaming and Health?

One of the newer trends in health care is the addition of gaming, such as Nintendo's Wii Fit, as a health care tool. Many people like to play video games and interactive games like this. Health care professionals are working with gaming companies to create video game-like activities to improve cognitive skills and change sedentary behavior. The results could also be used to measure things like blood pressure and oxygen levels as well. Who knew that a video game could be so productive and good for your health?

Try It Yourself!

How quickly does a disease spread? And how many people are affected by this spread? It is sometimes hard to imagine how quickly and efficiently a disease or infection can spread. That is why scientists and health professionals use computers. Try this short activity with your friends to see how an infection can quickly get out of hand and why computer programming has changed the way we understand diseases.

Materials:
- two small plastic cups for each person
- water
- marker
- granular dishwasher soap
- phenolphthalein

1. Each person should get two small cups. The more people you work with, the more dynamic the demonstration will be. Consider enlisting the participation of your entire class at school or scout troop or team.

2. Mix up one "contaminated" solution by adding a small amount of dishwashing power to water in one of the cups. Hand this to one person. Everyone else gets one cup of plain water and one empty cup.

3. Approach others in the room. Pour a small amount of their cup of water into your empty cup and mix it with your plain water. Test your cup with phenolphthalein. You will see a change in color if you have a "contaminated" sample.

4. Keep track of how many people you come in contact with.

5. Continue this until you get a "contaminated" sample. Record how many people you had contact with.

6. Continue until everyone in the room has been "contaminated." How long did it take? What does this tell you about the spread of disease?

5

COMPUTERS IN THE MEDIA

One rainy afternoon, Mr. Dewey showed his seventh grade computer class an old cartoon. It was the short, black-and-white cartoon with Mickey Mouse called *Steamboat Willie*. Made in 1928, *Steamboat Willie* was the original Mickey Mouse cartoon. His students enjoyed it but looked a little confused when Mr. Dewey turned on the lights.

"Uh, that was fun, Mr. Dewey. But what does this have to do with our class?" Chloe wanted to know.

"Glad you asked. This was the original Mickey Mouse cartoon. Describe to me what you saw."

Hugo raised his hand. "Well, it was pretty basic. And sort of choppy. It was almost as if each scene were cut out of paper or something and then all spliced together."

"I agree. That's totally what it looks like. And you are pretty close to being accurate. This was early technology in the film industry. Here is what it looks like today."

Mr. Dewey turned the

Words to Understand

CGI Computer-generated imagery: term for pictures and video used in film created by computers

pixels the individual building blocks of a digital image

resolution the amount of pixels a particular video screen can show at one time; the more pixels shown, the sharper the images

lights back off and brought up a clip of the movie *Toy Story 3*. "Now this film came out in 2010 and most of you have probably seen it. *Toy Story 3* was made with **CGI** technology—or computer-generated imagery. Most of the cartoons out there are made this way."

The students laughed at the short clip of the film before Mr. Dewey turned the lights back on. "What difference did you see?"

One of the students raised her hand. "Well, things were much smoother than they were in the Mickey Mouse film. And it looked very real. You almost could believe that those were real dolls and toys moving."

Around the world, movies created with computer-generated imagery and digital animation have been blockbusters.

Flight Simulators

Computer animations and graphics have many applications. One is in the world of flight simulators and pilot training. It's difficult to have pilots safely experience a number of emergencies that can occur during flight. A computer-based simulator is one way for this to happen. As technology advances, so do the tools that can be used for educational purposes. The scenarios become more and more lifelike and our future pilots are better trained.

"It's all about pixels," explained Mr. Dewey. "Before you ask, pixels are picture elements. They are small dots that make up an image. They are bits of color that are programmable on a computer display or in an image. The size of a pixel is determined by the resolution of a screen."

Hugo leaned over and whispered to Chloe, "This is what I've been afraid of all this time. All this talk is too technical for me."

"Oh come on," Chloe whispered back. "You have to admit when you use this technical language in reference to movies, how bad can it be?"

Mr. Dewey and the students talked some more about the movies. "What about other forms of media? Where else are computers used?"

The students began a list of computer images in the media. Many students commented that computer graphics were used in the news programs they had seen. One student mentioned how a computer graphic of a recent plane crash had caught her eye because it looked very realistic.

Hugo raised his hand. "I saw a weather report where a satellite image of a hurricane was animated. That is an example, right?"

"Absolutely. And these computer graphics are not just for show. Computer modeling is used as a tool—for everything from predicting the weather to diagnosing cancer. There is more to it than just movies."

"It's not Mickey Mouse stuff, is it?" laughed Chloe.

Try It Yourself

Time-lapse photography takes a series of still photos and strings them together in rapid succession to form a moving image. You could do that with a camera. Or you could make your own time lapse "movie" with a pencil and notebook.

Materials:
- small pad of paper or notebook
- pencil and eraser

1. Decide on your "movie" theme. Are you going to draw a series of pictures to show two people racing, a cat jumping off a tree, or a skier jumping off a ramp and tumbling into the snow? The possibilities are endless. Start with a very simple scene with only one or two images in the scene. This will make it easier as you become used to the process.

2. Start with the very first scene. Draw the small image along one edge of the notebook.

3. On the next page, alter the scene or image ever so slightly. For example, you might want to have a character's arm move from his waist to over his head. Keep in mind that the smaller the changes, the more detailed your overall "movie" will be.

4. Continue until your scene is complete.

5. Hold the notebook by the spine and run your thumb along the edge of the paper to animate the scene—it's a flipbook. Do you see it? Did you make a good "movie?"

6
FACIAL RECOGNITION

"Today," Mr. Dewey announced, "we enter into the world of espionage and top-secret security. We're going to talk about the way that computer technology has changed the way we see people."

His class had his full attention at this point. It wasn't often that teachers spoke so **cryptically**.

"Consider this," he continued. "People have always been able to recognize and distinguish faces. Not always with 100 percent accuracy, but most people certainly recognize others that they have seen before. But computers haven't been able to do that until recently. In the 1960s, scientists began to work with programs that could recognize human faces. Only recently has this been effective."

Mr. Dewey held up a picture of a man. Then he held up a picture of a crowd of people. "If you were given this picture of a person and allowed to study it for a while, you might be able to pick him out of the crowd."

Hugo muttered to Chloe under his breath, "It's *Where's Waldo* all over again."

Words to Understand

cryptically expressed in a secretive or hard-to-understand manner

data points individual pieces of information that can be examined together to find information or arrive at a conclusion

Mr. Dewey heard him and agreed. "Yes, it's like *Where's Waldo*, but we aren't looking for a guy in a striped hat, we are looking for this man's face.

"Each face has landmarks that make it unique. Your eyes and your brain register these landmarks as you stare at the picture. The idea was to make a computer program that could look at those landmarks as well."

"What landmarks?" a student wanted to know.

Mr. Dewey said, "Well, things such as the distance between the eyes. Or the width of the nose. Other things include the depth of the eye sockets, the shape of the cheekbones, and the length of a jaw line. These are all things that computer programs are now able to recognize."

Hugo raised his hand and asked, "I just don't get it. How does that help identify a criminal or a missing person?"

"Think about this." Mr. Dewey explained. "A computer scans the face of a woman robbing an ATM. The scan gets information about the distance between her eyes, her jaw line, and the other things I mentioned."

Chloe interrupted to ask, "But what if she is wearing a wig or something?"

"But the computer doesn't look at her hair," Hugo said, getting what Mr. Dewey was saying. "The computer looks at things she can't change that easily."

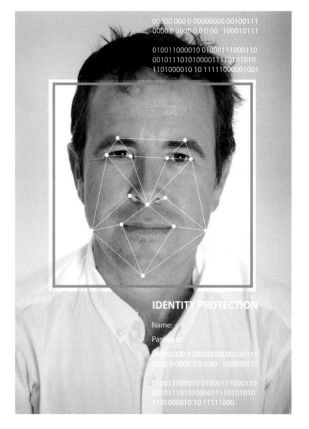

Computers "read" faces by capturing key landmarks.

Biometrics

Facial recognition is part of the science of biometrics. Biometrics are ways of identifying an individual using unique physical characteristics—in other words, using a person's unique biological traits to identify him or her. These traits include not only facial structures, but fingerprints, eye scans (right), and voice. Technology has improved and is making the use of biometrics a useful tool in identification.

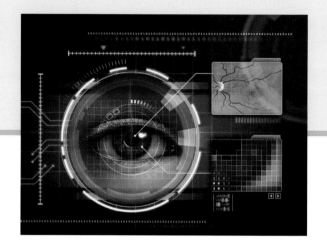

"Right," the teacher said. "And now the computer has those **data points** and that information. Her facial features are registered in a database. And the police can use that to scan the faces of people in a crowd outside of the bank. Or in the coffee shop down the street. Or anywhere. They will be looking for her. They can generate posters to send to the media and the public."

Another student spoke up. "They can use that information to scan a crowd of people to see if she is there?"

Mr. Dewey nodded and said, "Yes. Of course, it's not 100 percent perfect, and it's not as if they can grab her right away out of a crowd. But they can use the technology to see if she is there and maybe track her. There are many ways to use it."

Hugo looked at the images on the screen. "It's getting more and more difficult to disappear these days." He realized everyone was looking at him. "Not that I was planning on robbing a bank or anything. It's just interesting is all."

Chloe laughed, "Don't worry, Hugo. We all remember your face, anyway."

Try It Yourself

Interested in facial recognition technology? How exactly does it work? Try this activity to see the steps that a computer must go through when trying to use facial recognition. You'll be very glad that computers are here–they make this process much easier!

Materials:
- photographs showing a face shot (school studio pictures work well)
- ruler
- pencil
- calculator
- graph paper

1. Some measurements on a face can't be changed very easily. It is possible to make some measurements on a face and use that information to identify the face later on.

2. Use a ruler and the school photograph to measure the following facial features: the distance between the eyes, width of the nose, depth of the eye sockets, shape of the cheekbone, and length of the jaw line.

3. Make a chart that features all the distances.

4. Compare this with the distances of another face.

5. Note the differences in the measurements that you find. How are people's faces similar in size? Where are some of the biggest differences? Look online for more articles on how facial recognition software works.

7
THE CLOUD

"How many of you have heard of the Cloud?" Mr. Dewey asked his seventh period computer class one afternoon.

He looked as most of the hands in the room shot up. "Okay, next question. How many of you know what the Cloud is?"

He slowly nodded his head as he watched hands go down, or remain half way up and half way down. "Ah-ha," he said. "That's about what I expected. Most of us have heard of the Cloud, but most of us aren't really sure what it is. So join the club."

Chloe raised her hand and asked, "Isn't the Cloud a place where data is stored?"

"Yes, that's exactly right." Mr. Dewey continued. "The Cloud is a place where data is stored. But it's sort of difficult to imagine."

One very shy girl in class raised her hand to ask, "Is it really like a cloud? Is it up the air?"

Mr. Dewey shook his head and said, "I know. I thought that, too. But it's not a big fluffy thing. It is a physical structure. Many, many large computers are located at places all around the world and they store our data."

"But why would we want to use that? Where are my data and my pictures and my emails?" Hugo wanted to know.

"Putting all that data into one place—the Cloud—is partly for convenience. It used to be that you needed a big computer with a lot of memory to store all your data. Sometimes, your computer would run out of room and you'd need to add more memory to it, such as with additional hard drives, for example. Or you would back your data up on these things—a floppy disc." He held up a thin, square box a bit smaller than a CD case.

Hugo raised his hand and laughed, "Oh, I've seen those things. I thought they were coasters! I saw them in some sort of touristy store once."

Mr. Dewey laughed along with the class. "Well, floppies are only good as coasters now. At one time, they were the state of the art of data storage. But with new advances in storage, no one really needs them anymore. But you can think of a stack of these as the very first 'cloud.'

"But nowadays, you almost don't need a hard drive. You don't need to store information on your physical computer. You can write a report on your desktop computer at home, head to the library with your laptop and access it from the place you stored it—the Cloud. You could then save it to the Cloud again and head to the coffee shop later and reread the document on your phone. This is what the Cloud has done. It is a place to store our data and our information so it can be used on many devices."

The Memory List

Computers store information as memory in the form of bytes, or individual pieces of code. The computer can read those codes as you are reading these words. It takes lots of letters to make a book and lots of bytes to make computer memory. Here are some key amounts to remember:

KB: kilobyte (1,024 bytes; about 100 words)

MB: megabyte (1,024 kilobytes; about 200,000 words)

GB: gigabyte (1,024 megabytes: about 250 large books)

TB: terabyte (1,024 gigabytes: about 1,500 CD-ROMs)

PB: petabyte (1,024 terabytes; nearly all the photos on Facebook)

Chloe focused in again on the location and asked, "And it is just a series of super big computers somewhere storing our data?"

"Essentially, yes," Mr. Dewey agreed. "You pay a company, like Apple or Google or Dropbox, to store your information, and in return they let you access it anywhere you can connect to the Internet."

"Is it safe?" Hugo asked.

"You've come up with the biggest question of all, Hugo," Mr. Dewey said. "Everyone is asking that question. And in fact, it's a question that is still being answered. There have been many well-known leaks of information from the Cloud. Photographs, documents, all those things can be accessed and then leaked or shared with others. There is concern about security to be sure. But experts are working hard to make it as safe as possible."

"Can you get away with not using it?" Chloe wanted to know.

"For now you can, but in reality, you probably already do use it. Emails, texts, and other messages are stored in the Cloud. There's always a risk. But it's the future of technology. It's tough to argue with that. Our future is in the Cloud."

The Future of the Cloud

The future of the Cloud holds more than just data and pictures. Scientists and programmers are looking to the Cloud for many other purposes. Potential applications include the use of the Cloud as a crime solving tool as pictures and videos can be used to find criminals and missing people. Biologists could tap into the Cloud to predict trends in biodiversity, as numerous studies from around the world are analyzed at the same time. There is a chance to improve disaster response, as the Cloud is used to detect earthquakes faster with the use of monitoring equipment and completion of information from social media. The possibilities are as wide as the virtual sky.

Try It Yourself

The Cloud is a very abstract concept. You can't see it. You can't touch it. And yet we all look to the Cloud to store our data. Many people have trouble understanding what exactly goes on in the Cloud, how to access it, and how to protect it. You can teach them!

Suggested Materials:
- pen/pencil
- paper
- markers, colored pencils
- poster board

1. Ask a few people what they know about the Cloud. What are they curious about? What about the Cloud makes them nervous? You might consider asking older adults who may be unfamiliar with it.

2. Use the Internet to research the answers. What other information could you provide someone so they could confidently and securely store data on the Cloud?

3. Create a poster or pamphlet that teaches someone all they need to know about the Cloud and using this tool. What did they think?

8
ROBOTS

During the last week of the term, Mr. Dewey asked his students to make a "wish list." On it, they were asked to list three things that they would want to use a robot for.

The lists were interesting. Almost everyone said they wanted a robot to help them with their homework. Other students asked for a robot to set the table, or clean their room, or feed their cat, or find their missing keys. Others wanted a robot to answer their phone and take a message or to tell them what the weather was like that day.

"You do realize, don't you, that robots are already a big part of many of our lives?" Mr. Dewey challenged.

Hugo and the other students were skeptical. "Well," Mr. Dewey said when he saw their faces, "how many of you have one of those automatic vacuum cleaners?" Several students raised their hands. "Does anyone have a robotic toy? Like a dog that can do flips or a droid that can respond to your voice?" Hugo had one of those and raised his hand.

Mr. Dewey nodded, "I thought so. Let's think about some practical uses of robots."

He showed them a photograph of a drone. "This is a security robot. It flies over a property to check for trespassers and fires and other dangers. They can be very expensive, but since they are able to transmit videos and photographs, it is a useful tool."

The next photograph he showed them was of a robot used by caregivers to communicate with patients. "This is sort of like an advanced baby monitor. Many of your families probably had one of these when you were young. This advanced robot is called a telepresence robot. It allows a patient, perhaps an elderly person living on their own, to interact with a nurse or caregiver. Perhaps the nurse can just check in to see how they are doing, or to remind the person to take their medication."

Chloe asked, "That would help people stay independent longer, wouldn't it?"

"Yes, it sure would," Mr. Dewey continued. "If any of you came to school in a car today, you were helped by a robot. The largest use of robots in the world today is in building things. Robots can do whatever they are programmed to do over and over without getting tired. They are used in factories to help make cars, computer chips, and many other products. Doctors can even use robots in surgery. The ability of robots to respond to commands lets surgeons use much smaller instruments, which means patients recover faster from operations.

"Of course, robots are all over science, from diving deep into the ocean to crawling around the surface of Mars," the teacher continued. "By creating machines that can act independently—based on instructions given by programmers—scientists are able to 'go to' places they had never seen before.

A nice game of soccer is just one of the thousands of ways that engineers are finding ways to use robots today.

Robots on the Go!

What if you are on vacation, and want to check on your cat who is home alone. This robot would allow you to do that, and possibly talk to him to make sure he is comforted. What if you wanted to go to a rock concert but it is in a city far away? Maybe you could rent a robot at the concert and experience the concert from the first row. The future of robots could allow you to be in many places at once. Places you might not be able to get to normally. Imagine what this could do for businesses and schools? It would be like Skype, only much better. And you could go places, like the Great Wall of China, instead of just reading about it in a book!

"You can even find robots in sports. There are many ways robots could be used in sports. In fact, there are examples now that robots are reporting on sports. Automated sports stories are happening now and are expected to become more and more prevalent in the near future."

"Automated sports stories? I don't get it." One student said.

"Well, think about a basketball game, for example. There is so much going on. There is so much high-quality data being generated about the players, the score, the stats. This data can be crunched and analyzed by a computer more easily than it can be done by a human. Some companies have taken that data, added a set of standard sports words and phrases, and programmed robots to generate actual sports stories. Some of them have fooled readers into thinking they were written by humans."

Hugo looked pensive "Hmmm. Could a robot write my science report? Sometimes we generate a lot of data in our lab assignments."

"Now, don't get me in trouble with your other teachers," Mr. Dewey said. "At this stage of your life, I think you need to generate your own reports."

"But some day," Hugo thought, "some day…"

Try It Yourself

What would your perfect robot do? What in your life could you use a robot for? Design your own. Who knows, maybe someday it will become a reality.

Suggested Materials:
- pen/pencil
- paper

1. Decide what you want your robot to do.

2. What will it need to have? What will it look like? Include dimensions and potential materials.

3. Who would want to use your robot? Could it help others? Create a marketing plan and advertisement for your robot.

Bonus: You can also find kits to build mini-robots. If you're able, visit an electronics store, a hobby store, or even a toy store. Check out the many products that let you create robots that you can even program. They might look and act like toys, but they are high-tech machines and a great way to get started on being part of the robotic future! Many of these robot kits can even be programmed using a language called Arduino, which is a very basic and easy-to-learn way to tell computers and robots what to do.

9
CONCLUSION

Computer Science. There is so much to think about when it comes to this topic. From the email or text from our friends, to the machines that diagnose our health issues, to the technology that takes the astronauts into orbit around Earth and beyond—computers are a huge part of our lives.

And it is strange to think about, but it hasn't always been that way. The science of computers is a relatively new science. Technology, and in particular computer technology, has grown by leaps and bounds over the past few decades. Advances seem to happen overnight. Kids born now can't imagine what life was like without the Internet or iTunes or texts. People like your teachers and parents are struggling to keep up with the new technology. Imagine what things will be like when you are older. Your iPhone will look like an old rotary dial phone (you can look that up on Google if you aren't sure what it looks like).

But with all this technology and all these advances come a new set of dangers and responsibilities. Protecting yourself, your identity, and the trust of your friends and family online can be very difficult to do. When using the Internet and various social media sites, it is important to stay safe.

Be sure to stay on top of your own online safety. Think about things like this. Make a list of all your personal information, like your first, middle, and last names, and your address, including your postal code. What about your age and date of birth or your family members and their birth dates? Who would you give that information to? What about photographs of yourself? Write down the people you would want to share this information with.

Then make a web. If you give your best friend a picture of yourself, who could they share it with? See how quickly that picture could get to ten people? To 100 people? What if you gave that same person your birth date and zip code? It wouldn't take long for 100 people to have that

Every connection you make online can turn into dozens more with just a few clicks. We have never been more connected.

Whether you use a laptop, a mobile device, a tablet, or even a desktop, there is no escaping the presence of computers today.

information. And that is information that could be used for not so innocent purposes. Make a few more webs with your information and you'll see how quickly things can get out of hand on the Internet.

The Internet and all of computer technology is exciting. It is opening a new world for us all. Enjoy it. Embrace it. Just use it wisely.

Computer Science 24–7: Concept Review

Chapter 1

Businesses and individuals often have a significant presence on the Internet. Being able to navigate around the Internet and use it as a communication tool is key. Could you do it?

Chapter 2

The automobile industry has grown to use computers in many ways. Some are obvious and some are groundbreaking. In this chapter, find out how computers have changed cars.

Chapter 3

What apps do you have on your phone or device? You can learn about how they are made in this chapter and, like Hugo and Chloe, even make your own.

Chapter 4

The health care industry has been changed forever with the use of computers. Find out more about how your health and well-being is impacted by technology.

Chapter 5

Hugo, Chloe, and the rest of the class discovered how computers have changed how we look at movies and the media in this chapter.

Chapter 6

Think about all the people you saw today. What did they look like? Can you remember their faces? A computer can.

Chapter 7

Do you know what the Cloud is? Find out more about it here in this chapter.

Chapter 8

Is there a robot in your life? You may have one for fun or for work. What would it be like to have your own robot?

FIND OUT MORE

Books

The Internet is your ticket to the world. There is so much to learn and find there. But it can also be a dangerous place. Are you confident you can stay safe online? This book has some very useful information—for boys as well as girls.
Cindrich, Sharon. *A Smart Girl's Guide to the Internet*. New York: American Girl, 2009.

Python is one of the most basic coding languages and the basis for many apps.
Lambert, Kenneth A. *Python Programming for Teens*. Boston: Cengage, 2014.

Maybe you like computer programming or are interested in learning a little bit more about it. Try this book. It is a great place to start.
McCue, Camille. *Coding for Kids For Dummies*. New York: John Wiley, 2014.

Web Sites

Want to see it? The very first Web page? It's still out there. Click on the link below—it's like going back in time. But don't expect any fancy graphics or animations. It's very basic.
info.cern.ch/hypertext/WWW/TheProject.html

Want to learn more about computers and coding? Check with your parents and look into some of the classes offered by this online service.
www.idtech.com/courses/

Think you know how the Internet works? Think again. There is more to it than just searching on Google! This site from Stanford University is a great way to go behind the scenes of the Web and the Internet.
Web.stanford.edu/class/msande91si/www-spr04/readings/week1/InternetWhitepaper.htm

Series Glossary of Key Terms

alleles different forms of a gene; offspring inherit one allele from each parent

chromosomes molecules within an organism which contain DNA

climate change the ongoing process in which the temperature of the Earth is growing over time

force in science, strength or energy that comes as a result of a physical movement or action

frequency number of waves that pass a given point in a certain period of time

friction the resistance encountered when an object rubs against another object or on a surface

gene molecular unit of heredity of living organisms

gravity the force that pulls objects toward the ground

greenhouse gases gases in the atmosphere that trap radiation from the sun

inertia tendency of an object to resist change in motion

laser an intensified beam of light

lift the force that acts to raise a wing or an airfoil

momentum the amount of motion by a moving object

semiconductor a substance that has a conductivity between that of an insulator and that of most metals

sustainable able to be maintained at a certain rate or level

traits characteristics of an organism that are passed to the next generation

wavelength a measurement of light that is the distance from the top of one wave to the next

Picture Credits

Dreamstime.com: Dolgachov 8, 42; Pixdragon 12; iQoncept 16; Derektenhue 17; Monkey Business Images 20; Aijohn874 24; chbm89 25; Evolution1088 26; Antonoparin 28; Franckito 29; Andreus 30; Nmedia 32; Bobitoshev 36; Theowl84 37; Naraytrace 40; Nasir1164 41.

Newscom/MCT/Staff: 21

About the Author

Jane P. Gardner has written more than a dozen books for young and young-adult readers on science and other nonfiction topics. She became an author after a career as a science educator. She lives in Massachusetts with her husband, two sons, plus a cat and a gecko!

About the Consultant

Russ Lewin has taught physics, robotics, astronomy, and math at Santa Barbara Middle School in California for more than 25 years. His creative and popular classes and curriculum include a hands-on approach to learning and exploring that instills a love of science in his students.

Index